The Chapter Before This One

Jalynne George

BookLeaf Publishing

India | USA | UK

Presentation by *BookLeaf Publishing*

Web: www.bookleafpub.com

E-mail: info@bookleafpub.com

ISBN: 9789363302969

First edition 2022

Dedicated to the me before you

PREFACE

In the story of your life, I hope this chapter closes and you find my name on the page that changed you.

STONES

A stone hurled into calm water sent ripples in all directions as far as the eye could see and beyond even the edges of that until they became imperceptible, but still exist.

What a careless act to toss a stone into the water and watch it sink. Who are we to disturb the delicate balance that lies beneath?

As we gaze across the untroubled expanse, we see only our own reflection. We cannot reach the depths, nor even glimpse them by standing on the shore.

So instead, we make an announcement- HERE I AM - and with careless abandon, send our missive,
heavy handed and defiant into the unknown.

We cannot reach the bottom.
We can watch as it breaks the surface and know that where it
settles the deepest part is changed until time and circumstance shift it once again.

This is how we cast our thoughts. Words flung in anger and pain, raining stones into the untold reaches of another's soul.

When they are released
can we ever gauge the magnitude of their impact?
A harsh word spoken pierces the heart and damages more than the eye can see leaving scars that fade until they become almost imperceptible, but still exist.

I stood at the water's edge and heaved with all my might. Was it the view of only myself that caused me to be so bold, so careless?

The stone sank.

The ripples expanded from the
center, further and further until they seemed to disappear. My reflection shattered and the peace that lay beneath.
I turned and walked away, but the wake continued
in my absence and it is rippling still.

SHADOW SELVES

I saw your shadow self
The one you always try to hide
I glimpsed you angry and petulant
Greedy with lust
A blatant manipulation
Immediately recognized
Turning me from you in that instant
And then I wondered
Was it there all along?

The side that I refused to see
Or coaxed out by humiliation
Wielding its ugliness in retaliation
But what about the tenderness
that you allowed?
The hope of my happiness
Was is it always up for trade?

Rarely was my guard lowered
Long enough to believe
the words you spoke
I needed action, proof
And do I have it now?

How quickly you turned-

a traitor
Or maybe that was me
I too showed my shadow self
And it was just as ugly
But only momentary
Not intentionally kept hidden
Controlled until provoked
Never justified
Inherent imperfection

Did we see only what we wanted?
Blinded by possibility
Tenaciously clinging to vestiges of hope
Is that my fatal flaw?
To take something hopeless
And project my indomitable will
Shall I call this temerity insanity
or something else?

We danced together in darkness
Inexorably linked
Our shadows intertwined
Hope and despair wed
Until the tremor passing through
tore us apart
Leaving ragged edges
We had tried in vain to seal

And so I saw your shadow self

The one you always try to hide
I glimpsed you wounded and alone
Greedy with want
A quiet helplessness
immediately recognized
Turning me from you in that instant
When at last I realized
It was there all along
A bottomless well
That I could never fill
A hunger that you cannot even name

I had wanted to share your pain
But you would not allow me
And in your pride rent from me
A vicious desire to strike
To hold the mirror up
So we could gaze together
At our own depravity
Our shadow selves
The ones we always try to hide

Fear, greed, calculation,
Vengeance, pride, humiliation,
Emptiness, lust, manipulation,
Loneliness, rage, rejection
The human condition
Shall I call this reflection insanity
or something else?

No, I will hold out for redemption
In my dreams our shadows are dancing still
Bound by relief of being known
Hope that refused to let us go
And in that instant loved

LOSING IT BUT ONLY FOR A MINUTE

Square pegs, round holes
When will I learn
I can't make them fit
No matter how hard
I try
Why do I sell
Myself short
and then when I
am spiraling out of control
Decide I am the one
With the problem
Forget that
If I wasn't taking
Two steps back
These things
Would never happen
Who ever heard of normal
Function
That is what I am looking
For
I do it rather well
Until I let you make
the rules
Silly tears

What am I crying for
I have my whole life ahead of me
Possibility still beats inside my chest
If I was going down
It would have already happened
Crazy definitely cannot sink this ship

I Am Not A Princess

In this life
I want someone to rescue me
Like the princess in the fairytale
But, there is no one
He's not coming
To sweep me off my feet
And I feel like I'm in hell
There is nothing
To wake me from this slumber
No pressing matter
To which I must attend
So, I close my eyes a few more hours
And I lie here in my bed
And my phone doesn't ring
Cause you don't call
And there is no one
To meet my needs, but God
And he feels so far away
There is nowhere to escape
I am trapped inside these walls
Inside the fear
Inside my head
And I wake up and I wonder
How much better
If I'm dead

I know that's not an answer
But, I pray for some relief
From this pain and from this life
So, I just go back to sleep
In my dreams
I can pretend that my prince
Is on his way
And I see the love I've waited for
We plan our big escape
I climb up on his dark horse
Cause white is not my thing
I gave up long ago in belief
In purity
I hold tightly to his back
And hide my tears
Where he can't see
And we ride and ride and ride
Then I wake up from this dream

FLAWED AND UNFINISHED

Realizing it's not a crime to leave this puzzle unfinished. Leaving the pieces I couldn't find to lie where they have fallen, under the couch with the dust bunnies, stale crumbs, and loose change. Finally letting go of the quest for perfection. Jagged edges, mismatched corners, a piece of sky where perhaps the reflection of water in a lake belongs. Finally accepting flawed and unfinished it began and flawed and unfinished it will remain

A WHISPERED I LOVE YOU

slow dancing, small circles
soft music I don't even hear
over the pounding of our hearts
lights out
your lips on my ear
close your eyes and imagine I am there
with you
breathe in my scent
raindrops and clean sheets
both leave you breathless
arms around me to keep me upright
for surely my feet now fail me
bereft of words
our bodies speak
in a silent, ancient language
lay me down next to you
my head on your chest
say nothing
but I hear
a whispered I love you.

RHAPSODY

I hear it call my name
I feel it in my veins
This rhythm in my blood
And it will never be enough
To keep it to myself
I hear it call to me
Beckoned by destiny
Whispering to my soul
Come to set me free
The moon, the tide,
The stars that light the sky
Orchestrated by an unseen hand
That set infinity
Into the hearts of man
And who am I to ask why?

I didn't even know that I was searching
But I hear it in the silence
Sometimes when all is quiet
Still it's there
In the patter of the rain
The sound of falling snow
This echo, always,
The same sweet refrain

What is this that I long for?
I didn't even know I was in need
It seems to be coming
From somewhere deep inside me
It starts in my toes and pretty soon
It's sweeping me off of my feet
The cadence of Angels
The sweetest melody
I'm sure you've heard it too-
In the cry of a child,
The twinkle of street lights,
The tinkle of wind chimes
It never stops calling me

LISTEN.LISTEN.LISTEN
I breathe in, I breathe out,
I hold my breathe
I let the music of creation envelope me
It has left me defenseless
It washes over me
A timeless symphony
A cacophony of thunder
Just when I was lulled to complacency
It reminds me why I'm here
Because If I ever stop this RHAPSODY
Then I will disappear!!

FIRST KISS

Days later
Sitting here
Eyes closed
Half a world away
Wishing I was where
You are
Feeling Heat
Like fire
Your hands
On my back
Burning holes
In my shirt
Your lips
On mine
Tasting you
Sweet like
Honey
Wanting more
Right now
Possibility beats
Inside my chest
Pushing fear
Away
Hoping I had
the same effect

On you
Knowing
If I didn't
Those may still
Be the sweetest
Kisses
I've ever known

WORDS

So many things to say
All at once
A million thoughts
Screaming for attention
Wondering
How it would be
To swallow them
One by one
Until I choked
On all the things I'll never
Get to say
If all my words fled me
And my fingers refused this
expression
Would I explode?

HOW COULD I NOT FALL

Pulled under by the tide
Of your charismatic life
You showed me I could live
You took my broken dreams
Into your hands
Like a magician
You made them new again
I faced my biggest fears
Found that I was wrong
You caught the tears
I'd been holding all along
Maybe from the start
You knew you'd let me go
But not before
You gave me back my hope

You're not Superman and
Sometimes strong men fall
I found that in the end
You couldn't risk it all
Love is strong
But reality is stronger
Only wishing now
You'd held on a little longer
No one said it would be easy

We told the truth from the start
Now I'm only wondering
What to tell my heart?

How could I not fall?
You arms were safe and strong and ready
I trusted you
I knew you'd catch me
For a moment, I believed I could have it all
So tell me
How could I not fall?

MORE THAN A LOVER

You were here and now you are gone as if I never
knew you. Funny thing, I remember every moment.
A smile, a laugh, a song. Like a favorite movie, they
dance behind my eyes, a hundred memories. I
could revisit them one by one, but like you I will
forget, though much more slowly. When I think of
you I smile. I wonder how it is that I have become
someone you never knew at all and I am sorry.
Whatever moment it was that caused this, I would
go back in time and capture it so it was never lived
and you were still here with me. Because I miss
you. Because even though you cannot see them
my tears still fall. I called you my friend and you
were right. That was what I needed.

More than a lover.

UNTIL THEN

You will find a hand to hold
Someone else will touch your soul
All that I am to you
Every good thing I do
What is now won't always be
But until then

It's me standing here
Drying all these wasted tears
Not gonna cry
One more time over you
What good would it do?
What is now won't always be
But until then

Wondering what she'll have
That could take my place
Will she make you laugh
When you look at her
Will you see my face
What is now won't always be
But until then

Fighting a future that isn't yet here
Knowing what we have soon may disappear

Until then be here with me
Until the day you set me free
Until my laugh doesn't echo in the dark
Until the day you give me back my heart
What we have now won't always be
But until then

Baby it's me

BY YOUR LIGHT ALONE

When the sun shines on me, I feel my self open
up from a long deep sleep and then it is cold
again
and with it confusion. To feel the warmth, to
drink it in, I have felt safe in the comfort of your
arms.

In the light, I have allowed myself to hope.
Should the dark come, I am ready, for I have
stood in the places where it is barren for so long
my thirsty heart could not be filled by your light
alone.

RUN

RUN, before it's too late
The tide that swept you up before
Is creeping at your door
Am I that weak that I would
Seek to save again what's lost?
I see parallel lines
Along this divide
It is deep and it is wide
Sometimes living on the edge is the
Only thing reminding me
I'm alive
Would I do it all again to find
How one heart can shatter
A thousand times before
It can never be restored
Or will I RUN?

THE ASCENT

I am standing with my face pressed to the cool
glass palms up, in the prison I made, created by
pain and circumstance. You are on the other side
just out of reach, tears streaming down your
face,
backing away. There lies a million hurts between
us and a valley so deep only the bravest would
ever dare to breach it.
In an instant I let down my wall. I created it,
surely I
can shatter it at will. It was built to keep hurt
out,
but here I am trapped by it instead. And so, I let
it
all go. It comes crashing down around my feet
and
I begin my descent into the valley, slowly down
one
side. With a white flag, I come. I have nothing
else
to offer you but this token of peace.
You and I are both suffering wounds inflicted by
the enemy. Remember…the enemy, I am not. I
want nothing in return. Only, that you begin the
descent down one side to meet me in the middle,

as friends. I am here to help you.

Only, to give you a hand to hold and comfort when
you are weak. To tell you that it is okay to hurt.
Take as much time as you need. Remember if you
need me, I am here, standing in the valley waiting
to begin my ascent. Hoping that maybe you will
hold my hand and walk with me to the other side.
Where there is freedom. From the past, from the
pain, from the regret.
To know that in the distance there is still hope, still
life, still love.
I think I will lie down in the green grass and make
angels while I wait. I will feel the sun warm me and
smell the scent of freedom as the wind carries it
across my face.

A STORY EVERYBODY'S GOT ONE

We shared betrayal today over cups of coffee.
Unveiling wounds gaping and raw, like a woman
without an episiotomy. You can sew her back up,
but it's never quite the same. You held my hand
as
tears splashed on my paper placemat. The
shadow
you saw pass over my eyes and the distance you
say I put between us was already there. It wasn't
a
shift, so much a suppression.
For a moment I forgot myself, and you
witnessed
the slip like a reflection in the mirror, a shadow
as
the clouds pass over the sun. For a fraction of a
second you witnessed my pain, carefully
concealed. A dam about to rupture, spilling its
contents in abject fury. A force once unleashed
that will never be contained again. I am not
ready
to face it. It will take more than I have. It will
cost
more to let it go than it does to keep it where is,

just below the surface.
If I let down my guard for just a moment, it flashes
in my eyes like the glint of the sun on the hilt of
a sword and it cuts you just as quick

Am I remiss
for saying no one could share my pain and go with
me to the depths that must be descended?
Do I
think too highly of myself that another soul no
matter how scarred could ever have shared the
same cup?
I think not. I have lived a thousand lifetimes in
only
a fraction of eternity. I have tasted loss so deep
words can never convey its existence.
So, I thanked you for breakfast instead. I wiped
my
face and picked up the trash I knocked to the
floor
when you found me out. I carefully avoided your
questions and kicked my self for what I let
escape
me. I do not want to be known by you.
Then what and to what end? Can you do
anything

to help me? What is the telling of a story? Mine is
just that, a story and everybody's got one. Who gives a f@#k?

NOTHING BLEEDS FOREVER

I don't want to know
If you can please me
I want to know
If you can make my heart
Speak again
Words long forgotten
Like shards of glass on my tongue
Bleeding in an instant
The moment I roll them around and try them out
For you
Telling you secrets
I gave up telling long ago
Hoping that you might understand
That you might not turn me away
In a moment of courage
I present myself open
And bleeding
Missing parts of me long held captive
Tumbling from my lips to your ears
Words on a page that hold me bound
Stitched together just by knowing
You have heard me
Wondering if you have the strength
To reply

To listen to my story
To tell me yours
To let the wounds heal
Nothing bleeds forever

HOPE CURLED UP TIGHT

Hope curled up tight in my belly
A rock sunk at the bottom of a deep well
Started to unfurl like a flower
After the storm has passed
In my chest, possibility beats
Humming quickly making me feel
Lighter than air
And what happens
If I bury this hope
Deep once again
Next time my heart doesn't beat as quick
My smile not as wide
and doesn't reach my eyes
So, should I leave that rock
Where it lies tightly clenched
Never letting go
Or should I open up to possibility
And let it carry me where it will
Higher and higher
Breaking the surface
Sucking in great gulps of freedom

THE GHOST IN THE NIGHT

I'm the ghost in the night when you turn out the
light…the heartbeat pounding beside you
I'm the voice that you hear…the one in your ear
when you are all alone now
I'm the whisper in the wind and the passion in
the rain and when the thunder comes you will
feel my touch again
I'm the face you can't remember and the
laugh you can't recall and one day you'll
remember that you once had it all

Bruises

Bruises blue in the sun
Marks you left behind
Evidence that you exist somewhere

www.ingramcontent.com/pod-product-compliance
Lightning Source LLC
LaVergne TN
LVHW051242200726

843510LV00011B/1651